The Tale Of My Mind:
As Told By Dan Fella

The Tale Of My Mind:
As Told By Dan Fella

2018

All words written by Dan Fella

Copyright © Dan Fella 2018

This edition first published in 2018

Cover illustrations copyright © Rishikant Patra

All rights reserved. No part of this publication may be reproduced, distributed, or transmitted in any form or by any means, including photocopying, recording, or other electronic or mechanical methods, without the prior written permission of the publisher, except in the case of brief quotations embodied in critical reviews and certain other non-commercial uses permitted by copyright law. For permission requests, write to the publisher, addressed
"Attention: Permissions Coordinator," at the email address below.

danny.fella@hotmail.co.uk

Printed by Lulu

First Edition

ISBN 978-0-244-67940-8

For Katie, my reason for waking
and the source of a million metaphors.

"Freedom is the way a bird flaps its wings, exuberant and flowing. Oppression is the way that we clip them"

DF

Contents

Foreword..1

Human Experience
- An Observation: Of Alcohol..4
- Marjorie...6
- Keep Me Here...7
- Mirror Maze..8
- The Human Experience..9
- Generation Gap...10
- Chance...11
- Maybe..12
- Coronation..13
- Ouroboros...14
- Expedition...15
- Anticipation Of A Kiss..16
- Ringside..17

A Lesson From Pain
- Reaper...20
- The Hourglass...22
- Head Prisoner...23
- Scarlet...24
- Still..25
- Climb With Me...26
- Why Do I Battle?..27
- Decomposition..28
- Avoid. The Void..29
- A Whole Year Ago..31
- Acceptance..32
- Sediment...33
- Implausible Heartbreak..35

Human Feeling
- Peripheral Activity...38
- 90's Child...39
- Spatial Deficiency...41
- Sonder...42
- Recurring Dream...44
- Restless Mind...45
- The Love Lost...46
- The Vortex...47
- Hollow Promise...48
- Sleep Paralysis...49
- Ersatz Fatherhood...50
- Palpable Fear...51
- The Choice...52
- Poetic Energy...53
- The Cliff...54
- Midnight...55

Inspiration
- The Inspiration...58
- Thought Droplets...59
- Metamorphosis...60
- A Hero...61
- The Dancer...62
- Binary Love...63
- Hell...64
- Starbucks...65

Anger
- Demonic Possession...68
- Unforgotten Enemy...69
- Unbroken...70
- Stranded...71

Love
- Aortic Mansion..74
- Snowed In..75
- A Letter To A Lover...76
- The Bridge..78
- My...79
- That Eye Thing..80
- Queen..81
- Understanding Love..82

Observations Of The World Around Me
- The Moor...84
- 45 Rockefeller Plaza..85
- Old Oak..86
- Whitby Harbour...87
- The Canal...88
- Humber..89
- The View...90
- Countryside...91
- A Single Willow..92

Weather And Seasons
- Winter Storm...94
- Winter Sun..95
- The Frost...96
- First Sign Of Spring..97

Feeling In Nature
- Floral Decay..100
- Like Bardo...101
- The Storm..102
- Urban Flourish...103

Imaginings
- Untitled..106
- Inky Black..107

x

- Sunset..108

Political Musings
- The Moral Of The Story.................................110
- Humandroid...111
- Closed Circuit TV Stars..............................113
- What-About-Ism...115
- The Wall...117
- The Model Citizen.....................................118

Social Outlook
- Anti-Social Media......................................120
- Air Trav-Hell...121
- Oh, Society..122

Tales Of War
- Waco..126
- Operation Tiger...128
- Syrian Nightmare......................................130

Comical And Lighthearted Poems
- To Be British For A Day............................134
- Man Flu...135
- South Circular...136
- Late Again...137
- How To Choose Your Tea..........................138
- The Snowstorm..139
- Adulthood..140
- The Commute..141
- Caught In A Pickle....................................142
- Mutual Friend..143
- A Chimp With A Paddle............................144
- The Boot On The Wire...............................145
- The Splinter...146

xi

Foreword

Human emotions and thoughts are very subjective. We can only directly see the world through our own eyes, anything beyond that is down to our own innate empathy. You see, we are limited that way as a species in that even though we coexist, we are still separate from one another. It is our own choice to love and to learn, to build and to grow. That's what makes us human.

The Tale Of My Mind sets out to demonstrate my own earthly findings. It is as much an explanation of my personal mindset as it is a description of who I am as a thinking machine. It outlines my flaws, my strengths, my triumphs, my failures and more importantly, it aims to pass on a learning experience. Now my worldly outlook is as totally unique as yours and there is every chance you will view this book as a collection of crap. The way that I deal with my inner problems and perceive those of others is totally up for question. And that is the point.

This is the tale of *my* mind and I hope that you can take something positive from it. I hope you can look at the way I think and feel inspired. I also hope that you will tell me where I am wrong and where I am failing so that I myself can continue to grow.

After all, we're all in this life together.

Thank you for reading.

Dan

Human Experience

An Observation: Of Alcoholism

The furniture took my hand as it span me round the room
In a spiral serenade through a blur of gloom.

The headboard took lead as I fell into its arms
Below a glitter ball ceiling that observed our dance.

A liquor fuelled vitality, neglecting morality,
A narcotic brutality, forgotten banality,

We swayed without motion in a paralyzed state,
While kaleidoscopic dreams preceded my fate.

I was too glazed to care that the feeling would lapse,
Of the torment when the inevitable crash wraps

It's hand round my throat in a distant morning,
And drags me from sanity without forewarning.

The glitter ball ceiling now seemed too close,
A claustrophobic nightmare induced by a dose

That I took to avoid the reality of life,
It seemed a worthy alternative to taking a knife

To my wrist, to carving the arteries there,
I never realised that my mental state would tear

When intoxicated thoughts took over my conduct
And that with each bottle the drug would abduct

My hope, my chances of improving any likelihood
Of growing, recovering a long-forgotten adulthood.

Now twelve months sober I can look back at a time
Where I religiously poured tears into bottles of wine.

I'm proud of the fact that I chose to give up,
That instead I opted to empty my cup

And find solace in real things – in life itself,
For I now have moral riches, unimaginable wealth.

Marjorie

A trunk stretches heavenward, gnarly weather-beaten limbs point up
Towards your sky.
Fir coated fingers poised in a prayer, swaying over a network of roots
That reach back to my childhood.

They are a memory ridden nervous system, breathing life into a
Hallowed ground you used to adore.
Our approach sparks a flash, one of a subconscious kind and electrical
Throbs surge throughout the three of us.
It is as though our interlinked hands conduct each memoir that flows
Through us like a circuit.

We walk forwards slowly, cumbersome at first.
A perfect sun watches down on us and we wonder if it is you, smiling
With undying pride at us all.
Board game cheater, stubborn old mule, a true survivor living on in our
Hearts.

You brought a special kind of light to this world; each person is unique
But you always managed to stand out.
The petals of this bouquet we placed upon the bough may rot to decay,
But your memory never will.

As those sun rays fall graciously onto the lawn around us I picture you
Holding out your hand like you always did,
Like you always would for anyone in need of it.
You never even mattered to yourself for that matter but to us you were
The only jewel in the crown.
A crown we still wear with pride every day in your memory, to
Remember your beautiful soul.

Keep Me Here

Contorted beauty, almost perfect but perfectly described.
Hung like that delicate moment between silence and the decision to scream.

Eternal entity, floating as an orb.

A loss of gravity. Slowly rotating without cessation.
A boat pedals sky, it's gangly feet hang under the hull, soaring.

Like a tide licking rocks, it could be gentle or an eroding rapture, who knows.
Juxtaposed danger and omnipotence

Like sliding your hand along a blade and remaining unscathed.
Untouchable, how could I be…

…Colour swept, arid landscape.

A mind map plotting the mind, intricacy explained; unravelled.
Elegance is a scary thing, as much as attraction is conceiving.

Fatal decisions encouraged by love.
Watercolour, gallons of ink, idea spawned blemishes I cannot unsee.

Or want to. I always want them here!
Scent from sound, accompanied by vision.

What I see is your creation, a sonic organism.
Beating, pulsing, ameliorating me.

Mirror Maze

I feel for the little man that runs around my mind, gathering ideologies and desperately trying to organise them, for my cerebral halls would be labyrinth enough even if they weren't mirrored.

A maze occupies my head, a reflective prison which winds and twists its way outward towards hellish cul-de-sacs. A Minotaur rallies against my protagonist, spoiling his challenge and halting his progress.

It leaves me so blinded and unable to make sense of my own thoughts and theories. The endless battle that is waged in my skull passage continues to dim my exterior senses and I am numbed to a world I don't understand.

But day after day that poor little man continues to battle against all odds. And despite his failings he habitually learns and gains strength after every mistake.

The Human Experience

We picture flowers growing as being beautiful.
The way the petals contort gracefully in the breeze.

We glorify mountains, imposing and looming like
A physical apparition, a creation to behold.

We visualize colour and marvel at architectural wonder
Whilst admiring fine food and wine.

We travel to far flung countries, we're impressed
By their culture and their foreign tongue.

We appreciate visual synergy and cinematic flair,
Wishing we were them, those actors whom we idolize.

But none of it can compare.

To me nothing could be more beautiful
Than the fervent way you love me.

Generation Gap

Floating on a cool spring borne breeze,
The ghost of juvenile laughter resonates dull.
These ancient playing fields seem so familiar,
Cast into my history, coercing memories to mull

Through my head, I imagine them unwrinkling my skin,
Forcing me to look back upon dreams that broke up.
I feel like a murderer returning to the crime scene,
Except my only infraction was growing up.

I can picture him roaming on a bicycle, smile fixed firm,
You see I killed that child, so innocent and free.
These old haunts remind me of that, that I wearily failed,
I could never achieve what I wanted to be.

Would he be disappointed if he could see what I became?
Or would he be happy that in his future I found love?
For although those childhood aspirations shattered,
I have a family now; forgive me, I have doubts to dispose of.

Chance

Drink from the tranquil pool, or is it a
Furnace?
Blurry eyes struggle to determine the
Texture.
The unknowing is killing you and maybe it will.

Alone in your struggle you're forced to
Decipher
And as you lower your lips towards the
Edge,
You feel a slight heat caress your face.

Soothing, welcoming; but is it
Fatal?
There's only one way to find the solution.
Dive in.

Maybe

Held in weathered hands,
Blissful precipice,
Cavernous void,
Mountainous appendage.
Could it be another chance to grow or impending melancholy?

Eyes enveloped in concern,
Retracted thoughts and pushed away doubt,

And stop.

Again, hesitation blooms,
Intertwined amongst a beating vein of affluence,
Bright in colour but dark in nature.

Weakening, waning,
It could be strong,
Maybe.

Coronation

As that crown is placed upon your head,
It's as though the precious metal begins to melt,
Liquifying and seeping over you like molten lava.

Inch by inch it embodies you, and power is
Moulded to your very skin.

Priceless stones embed to your skull and still
The amber falls ever nearer to a ground
On which inferiors tread.

Upon impact with the cool stone a thick steam arises,
Cloaking you, leaving you completely out of reach,
Blinded to our needs.

You cannot see our struggle for we suffer at the periphery
Of your celestial haven.

So, throw your omnipotent arms aloft and tell us you care,
But all we see is an impenetrable castle sat in cloud.

Ouroboros

Unify all in a serpentine stroke,
An ouroboros cycle beginning from end.
Consume oneself to learn how to live,
A necessary evil from which you descend.
Devoured by death, life comes to a close,
Defenceless to a fate with which it must fend.
Nature's fine order where opposites align,
We must do what we can before we ascend.

Merge hate into love and fear into trust,
Delve deep into mystery and begin again.
Vanishing entity masked from our view,
Maybe existing in Schrodinger's domain.
Thespian lies tell of perfect worlds,
But generations flourish and perish the same.
A phoenix from ash we arise once more,
A reflection of the past, standing in flame.

Expedition

Caught in a crosswind, a vapourless lull,
We struggle to pay our debts.
Force a foot forwards, traverse frozen wilds.
Hold the rail and let your hand scrape,
Ignore how your skin feels so raw.
And just hope, for a day when all your fears
– your pointless fears –
Seem so far, far behind that you'll break free,
Begin to see that you could be fine.
Because you could
Be fine.

Illusion of decline, hallucinatory hillside,
Place down your ropes and picks.
Your own propaganda has led you
To place that cliff face in your mind.
But it's superfluous, unnecessary,
It doesn't even exist!
Instead walk
Over a horizontal landscape;
In fact scratch that, run! Let frozen air hit your face,
Allow it to fill your nose and your throat
And your chest and lungs
And more importantly than anything else,
Survive!

Anticipation Of A Kiss

Slouched behind a steering wheel in an autopilot stupor,
Drifting through lanes as the miles blur by.
Tail light retina burn subliminally scars
While a warm sun settles below an auburn sky.

I've been driving for hours in a repetitive lull,
Lonely and vacant, my patience waning.
It's hard not to focus on the memory of your face,
Separated from you, I feel my willpower draining.

I can grasp it! So strong is the memory of you,
You're with me, my immaterial faraway muse.
Ghost lips are pressed deftly and smooth against mine
As I count down the minutes like a simmering fuse.

Subliminally caressed I can taste your spark,
Your radiant glow that I have grown to love.
I crave your reality, I long for your physical kiss.
I'm tortured and anguished by its lack thereof.

Ringside

I will never be a man like these other men,
With full stature looming and weather aged face.
Undeveloped and fragile I remain static
At the edge of the ring, lesser than them,
A glass finished supporting structure
Surrounded by steel beams.

Do you notice the fractures as they splinter?
Or do the cracks remain too hairline to see?
Sometimes I feel as though it is inevitable.
That surely those subtle cracks
Will give in and shatter.
Would you still love
The fragments of
Sand?

18

A Lesson From Pain

Reaper

That night I lay still as though frozen to the spot,
My arm hanging limply and my skin pulled taught.

A warm trickling liquid oozed to the floor,
As a reeling agony chiselled to my core.

I could not escape the ropes that locked me down, tied by a reaper,
With my face ablaze, I felt my heart sink deeper.

I was latched there, awaiting an imminent death,
As he leant across me smiling, with haunting breath.

It was an inhumane torture, fragmenting my very vitality,
I could not withstand the mental brutality.

The illusory ropes on my wrists left incisions,
Red like the corners of my bloodshot vision,

Carving crippling pain memories deep into my skin.
I broke down from ache and anguish, I could but give in.

I pled "Lead me away, my time here is done,
Take me from a planet where depravity has won."

The reaper's smile widened as he gripped my hand
And I felt my world swell like a cancerous gland.

Everything I loved appeared by my side
And upon realising what I had, I broke down and cried.

I was leaving a life to which I'd been blind,
I'd ignored the love and watched only pain unwind.

But now it's too late, as my ghost watches you suffer.
I love you so much, my poor grieving mother.

I took my own life in a blunt careless act,
I never anticipated such colossal impact.

Forgive me for making my final mistake,
I'm eternally sorry for making so many hearts break.

The Hourglass

Buried in sand by choice or by force, I'm unsure which.
Muscles weakened by their lack of movement.
Constriction is the strongest emotion, perpetual shortness of breath.
Helplessness I suppose, a demeaning vulnerability.

Grains of that same sand tumble ever closer to the funnel,
Dragging me with them, leading me to realise
Time is running out, slipping away into an unknown void.
What I will find there I do not know, but I know that I fear it.

An unknown future, the only certainty being impending
Loneliness, implosion, nothing, who knows?

But then everything changed with a single decision…

I sought help. And it was there! Cascading all around me
Like a glacier in Spring, restored to the roaring falls it once was.
Gravity fed, lifesaving sustenance, plunging upon
What once was drought, what was slowly asphyxiating.

A fish out of water suddenly flooded,
Once a lost cause, but now fighting for a cause!
Friends, family, family friends. A whole army of hope.
Why was I so blind before, so unwilling to see?

That despair can be conquered, need not be battled alone.
Together we row, down this stream that we helped flow
And I stand at the helm screaming euphoric,
For I see the harbour in the distance, safety from the storm.

Head Prisoner

I'm shaking alone in this derelict basement,
Locked from the outside, I'm trapped
Here with my own demons as cell mates.
They whisper in my ear, they torture my mind,
But as I throw my fist toward them,
It only passes through their putrid form.
Bars of natural light lay across my face
From between cracks,
A hint of a better world, outside my musty grave.
Blood hardens within scratches in the floorboards,
Matching the deep cuts in my fingertips,
Futile effort invested by nails bitten right to bone.
My heart is incarcerated by my own ribcage,
Locked into place by arterial manacles
That pump decaying thoughts to my extremities.

But I have air in my lungs so I could scream for help!
I cup my hands around my mouth and inspire hope!
I feel it rising like fire,
My blood is like fuel for the blaze.
Then footsteps creak in a foreign hallway,
And there's a chink as an axe is swung aloft,
Smashing into the rusted padlock holding me hostage
And freeing my conscience
From a tormenting purgatory.

Scarlet

I sat and felt them pulsing like a roadmap to my heart,
Weaving in scarlet, like they were plotting a star chart
Through the freckles on my arm, with a warm caress,
Heightened by a burgeoning sinkhole of stress.

So delicate they seemed, as they twisted around bone,
Such fragile threads with their blue tinted tone.
Our remarkable creator must have had so much trust
To place such a weak entity amidst our internal bloodlust.

As I stared at them meander I felt pounding in my ears,
One slash of that blade could have ended my fears.
I'd watch that scarlet pour out like uncorked wine,
A copper-like river, relieving my lifeline.

Yet memories swim, unhappy at first,
Flashing by my eyes like a flaring solar burst.
Epiphany thoughts remedied my negative judgement,
Reminders of love started to cure my mental ailment.

I dropped my blade to the floor and listened as it reverberated,
Shrill noise bouncing from walls in the room where I incarcerated
My inner demons, the sound completed an era in my mind,
The end of my suffering, the day I left my misery behind.

Still

Unseen, unfelt, suffering in silence, washed in
A daytime darkness, daybreak barred by a blackout blind.
Birdsong chime; the repetitive din of chronic life,
A monotonous tick as unseen clock hands unwind.

Terrified thought process, skull-walled purgatory,
Confinement for the monsters that roam through grey matter.
Plucking at nerve endings, slicing new scars,
Habitual depravity, like a flood borne from gradual rain patter.

Immobile, lifeless, restrained and yet free,
The only motion is the shake of my hand.
Afraid of the consequences of facing the day,
Instead of fighting I choose not to stand.

A nightmarish reality ensues in my head,
A fine-crafted fiction that twists my dying will.
Depression is the author that narrates my affliction,
Scribing a million metaphors for how I lie here so still.

Climb With Me

How can you see beyond a mountain without first climbing to the top?

Ocean floors are submerged between perpetual fathoms of shimmering constraints.
They can be bested.

Sun blinded by a love unseen,
Dark hallways cannot be navigated.
I am alone,
Wandering aimlessly as unknown hands close in.
Words get harder to find,
A world dead to a plea,
A night that won't end,
Rife with nothing.
No-one,
Nowhere,
Except...

An ignition of belief.
A memory of feeling creeps by and what was surreptitious hope becomes a spark,
Igniting this narrowing corridor with colour and revealing a mountainous slope!
Finally,
Gratefully,
I am climbing.

Why Do I Battle?

I hate to admit that my head is a mess.
A mêlée of storm clouds, an elegant wreck.
I can't seem to fathom the way that I smile.
How do I do that when inside I frown?
But the fact is I question the way that I am.
A massacred heart with no escape plan.
A source of blinding darkness, a bricked over well.
Trapping my victims inside with no help.
The voices of loved ones scream out from my hell,
Bathing in acid rain cast from my clouds.
They're tortured by godlessness while I watch on
With my head in my hands knowing not what to do.
Each terrified cry feels drawn out by my hand.
I never meant to tether them to my wrists,

Shackled in the same chains that drag me right down,
Slicing the skin there and leading straight below.
What's left of my damp hope still lingers on.
Praying for exile so that they be free.
Help clear my vision and remove smeared fog
That blinds me and blurs a truth I can't see.
I can change this, if only I could smash
Through the wall.
With hammers and picks
I begin to exert my energy, my morale,
I do this for them. A fragment of light starts
To burst through the bricks and shines onto faces
I'd kill to protect. For the first time my wry smile
Starts to make sense. I'm not alone in this world,
Finally I can speak in the future tense.

Decomposition

Vertebrae shattered like fragments of a mirror,
Infringed by a blade decayed by its bearer.
I don't want excuses, unravelling chronology.
I don't need apologies, useless analogies.

Sentimental calligraphy never felt so futile,
Scribing letters in bold font while ink goes out of style.
Kill me with tardy kindness after spite has pierced my soul.
Helplessly attempt to piece together a cavernous hole.

A razor wire cure stitched right through my skin,
Holding me whole but slashing organs within.
You don't see the damage caused by your spite.
To survive, my body faces a constant internal fight.

I imagine rusted hooks holding my head aloft,
Clawing at corporal mass and leaving scars embossed.
Memory marked tissue is a perpetual relic
Of a time well before the candle burned out its wick.

Before, I knew pain and was bludgeoned by grief,
But day after day I still sigh with relief
When I remember I'm human and this is how we all feel,
Pain and happiness are both equally real.

Avoid. The Void.

There is a strange beauty to be found in loss.
Right there in that moment between happiness and the realisation
That something terrible is about to happen.
Caught in a fragile balance between joy and sorrow,

Unfeeling, numb, alive, constricted and yet free.
You know reality will return to weigh you down,
Like a hand grasping your scalp and throwing
Your head below water onto rocks.

But in that brief second you care not.
You know not of feeling and of pain and of misery.
You know not of what you will feel momentarily.
Of course then it hits, there is never enough time to prepare,

To get yourself ready for that slap around the jaw.
The gaping wound that will surely appear in your chest,
Tearing out the best in you and laying it on the flagstones.

For you have lost.

That momentary beauty is gone, replaced by hideous pain.
A crippling courtroom callously sentencing you to life on death row.
A tunnel with no end, no light, why fight?
Why fight something you know has you beaten?

Because of hope you fool, because of hope that's why!
Are you forgetting we've all felt this way?
We've all been left alone, with no way of climbing
Out of the sinkhole caused by rains of despair

And yet we all escaped, we grappled and grasped,
Clinging at nothing, perilous and toxic air

Until we resurfaced and found ourselves home.

The pit is still there oh God knows we acknowledge that,
But truth be told we got over it, we learned
To put the pain on ice, to revisit at our leisure.

We learned to survive and so will you.

A Whole Year Ago

One year ago, the wounds bled constant.
Twelve months ago, to breath was to hurt.
Fifty-two weeks ago, I cradled my endurance,
A lifeless lost entity for which I'd given up hope.

A numbness seemed to fold itself around me
Like a chill, a blowing breeze tapping against my skull.
Even in the loving warm arms of an adoring family,
Even with everything I knew not how to cope.

My blackened vision cast a thick filtered hue,
Like staring through tar and feeling forced to swim.
Why make the effort to wade through the gunge?
When it seems so much easier to tie a loop in a rope?

So that's why when you tell me you love me I feel
Like an angel's wings are spread right before me.
Each word you utter is like a stitch to the gashes
In my skin, in my heart; my hardships elope.

Exorcised demons are easier to manage,
No longer controlling my inner most thoughts.
I place my trust in what I never thought possible.
You. You give me a future, a life with full scope.

My mother was right, there is more than fear,
More than a sadness that engulfs every cell.
Take my hand darling and lead me away,
Together let's begin to ascend that steep slope.

Acceptance

Like the sensation of fingernails on skin.
Stroking, scraping, scratching, scathing.
We cannot know the level of damage done,
    Until we observe.

And we cannot learn to heal the wounds,
    Until we accept.

       They exist.

Sediment

Imagine a rock face crumbling slowly. You know
It takes time for the sediment to chip away from the cliff.

Sandstone is a fine substance. Small, dusty particles
Gradually fall away and drift aimlessly, lost,

Without you even noticing their absence.
But as time passes you notice the change in formation.

The way that cliff seemed to bulge and burst
Proud and true, boasting sturdy structure

Has changed. It's different now. It still stands,
But you can't quite remember how it was

When you first found it, stood so ominously.
It's different now. Those particles are in the wind.

No matter how hard you search and you scream
For an easy fix, a way to restore its former glory,

You know that it's futile. There is no way,
They were lost along the way, it's way out of reach.

It's pointless to try and rebuild what was,
You have to accept that it has changed.

The cliff face you traversed has crumbled and slid,
The pathway you once strolled on is lost to the sea.

But the view is the same. The same waves crash into
the footing. The same sunshine blissfully falls

Upon you, enlightening you, that much is the same.
Seagulls still cry as they circle around your head,

Desperate for any loose morsel of food they can steal.
Steal a thought for what you still have.

The landscape may appear different, but what you loved,
What you dearly loved and adored remains.

Implausible Heartbreak

I never knew it were possible to
Love someone so much that a simple
Argument is heart breaking. Unsure
If this is a learning curve or a torture
Method, I can feel the panic rising
And the pain grows. If the eyes are
Windows to the soul, then why when
I close them does my spirit feel so
Exposed? As a blade runs down my
Inner psyche, splitting the very follicles
And capillaries one by one, I feel shut
Down, breaking piece by piece.

The steel continues to slash and I realise
This is a punishment born from my own
Self-doubt. I never trusted myself
Enough to realise what was staring me
Right in the fucking face.

It is love that wields the knife, trying desperately
To make me see that you give a fuck about
Me! For so long I have sat in peripheral
Vision and imagined myself failing. Failing
Myself, failing you. And yet I have you!

You are here in the flesh and the sooner
I look back at you and see adoration instead
Of disappointment, I can finally give you
Everything you deserve. There is no history
Reflected in those eyes, instead I see a
Billowing future. I need not fear you walking
Out of my life, or the terror of hurting you.

Upon this thought the bindings unshackle,
And a medicinal pill cures my malady…

…Or maybe it is just your lips.

Human Feeling

Peripheral Activity

A steady stroll in a commonplace neighbourhood,
A faintly uttered hum drifts on the wind.

A sonic flow, infiltrating your bloodstream,
Medicating a rhythmic disease, healing.

Lacklustre avenues devoid of any thrill,
Restored to glory by unbroken acoustic joy.

Animating darkness, rejuvenating monotony,
It brings out the best in a hopeless locale.

The sound licks the ground and bounces from walls,
A sound that only you can hear.

A whole world forgotten, irrelevant in an instant,
For that peaceful soundtrack is all that you need.

90's Child

As trees sway and clouds billow, reminiscence falls instead of rain.
I pull down my hood and allow the deluge to engulf me.

As droplets tug at my eyelashes and my vision begins to blur,
My perception transcends into memory.
The world begins to grow, seen through childlike eyes…

The trees are now climbing frames,
Not just photosynthetic tools.
The flagstones are a canvas for chalk,
Not just a commonplace commute.
My eyes are drawn into my surroundings
Instead of the six-inch screen in my hand.
They dart between the jumpers curled up
In a pile, ersatz goalposts laid out on the ground,
Before blazing with elation upon spying a stream…

We pedal in freefall down a steep hill,
Falling headlong over handlebars in a tumble.
The fire in my kneecap is the tell-tale sign of a graze,
Laughed off as we limp towards the woods.

As I blink the image shifts with a camera-like click
And I am thrown into a school playground.
I watch spades dig and dirt displace while
A silver capsule lies on the ground, surrounded by
A horde of babbling infants;
Each one carrying a possession,
A cherished artefact of their choosing.

Upon scanning the group, I spot long forgotten treasures,
Evocative of times gone by.
I see VHS tapes, marbles, catapults,

Conkers, books and gel tip pens.
Play-Doh, roller skates, Lego bricks,
Walkman's, Beyblades and Polly Pocket toys.

As the capsule was lowered to be discovered
By a future generation's eyes,
I wonder if they knew what they were really burying.
Not just the traces of their own childhood,
But the remnants of a pre-digital age.
The reality is, the remains of a world full of freedom and joy,
Became entombed inside that hollow tin shell.

It is then that I notice the ghost of my own juvenile memory,
Stood to one side with my naïve eyes beaming a hope
That the future I was promised will come to be...

Instead, as my mind whips back to the present
And I take heed of the modern world around me,
Men and women and children alike stare not at their setting
But into a barricade of pixels,
Glued to a live stream of irrelevance.
The streets are devoid of laughter now that
Handlebars have been replaced by gamepads.
It seems enjoyment can only be fulfilled indoors.

Why can't we draw our eyes from our devices for just two minutes!
Just for long enough to see that everything we ever wanted
And dreamed about has been thwarted by our own selfish greed.

Exponential progression has allowed technology to flourish,
But it seems that our mindset couldn't keep up.
The curse of being young in the 90's,
Is that we can still remember that feeling of hope.

Spatial Deficiency

The spaceman walks to the edge of the cliff,
Slams his flag into the ground and stares
Longingly at constellations he used to inhabit.

He climbed this mountain to gain as much altitude
As possible, desperate to be as close to his true home
As he can be. He dreams of lassoing the moon and stars,
Of pulling them closer back to him, where they belong.

As he shuts his eyes the planets revolve. He feels his feet
Lift above a world where drama and chaos engulf him.
But as he opens them again he sees that gravity won,
He remains tethered to a rotting earth.

If only he were as liberated as he were up there,
Surrounded by a vacuum of peace.

If only he could glance back at a marble planet,
Too distant to perceive war and poverty.

If only he could drift in an endless ether,
So insignificant in an ocean of black stretching far beyond
The imagination of even the most accomplished writer.

If only he felt free.

Sonder

I was sat alone on a park bench
Watching the world pass,
With a book by my side,
My eyes open wide...

I am a writer.
I pride myself on my ability
To perceive, to believe.

I see the child riding past
On a bike to my left,
While to the right
A woman flicks her hair
Elegantly over her shoulder.
Nothing evades my gaze
As I scramble for inspiration
In a world where
I am never short-changed.
There is beauty in every detail.

But it only took a moment
For the realisation to strike.
That I can barely see anything at all!

The world is like the sea
And all I can perceive
From my tiny island
Are the crests of waves
And the ships that pass across them.
I cannot see the fathoms
Beneath, where there may be
Beautiful coral,
Or deadly creatures

That tear the flesh
From fellow aquatic beings.
I cannot visualise
The terrors that haunt
The darkened caves and fissures
Or the danger of currents
That drag across oceanic swell.

I cannot even picture the tide.

They call it sonder
And for the first time
I truly understand its meaning.
All I see of the people around me
Is *their* surface.
A tiny fragment of who they are.
Why do they smile? Why do they cry?
Each and every one of them
Has their own tale to tell
And their lives
Are as equally intricate
As my own.
They feel the same pain,
Suffer their own problems
And live in a mind
As vivid and complex as I do.

Upon this realisation
My mindset changed.
I thought I had seen it all,
But the reality is
There are still seven billion
Untold stories to tell.

Recurring Dream

At night I pull teeth from my jaw one by one.
I can't help but to flick at them with my tongue.
It's as though the very bones are beginning to soften,
Laid out to rest in a fictitious wood coffin.

I begin to choke as I swallow the fragments,
Helplessly forced down my throat in banishment.
They tear at my chest and rest in my guts,
I feel blood in my mouth from a thousand cuts.

I open my lips to formulate a scream,
But it seems as though failure is a recurring theme.
Although from deep in my lungs air is rushed,
A vacuum ensures that my desperate pleas are hushed.

Restless Mind

With my eyes barely closed I hear a faint scratch,
Like a feral cat's claws upon wood.
My pupils dilate as they're suddenly exposed
To a horror washing over like a biblical flood.

Materialised thoughts are etched into my ceiling,
The jagged edged characters imprinted there.
As a fine dust rains down and envelops my face,
I can't help but lie motionless and fervently stare.

As the invisible scalpel continues to carve,
I read in a loop as though doomed to think.
My psyche is a weapon that leaves permanent marks,
They're burned into my eyelids with every blink.

Like an ancient text I am compelled to decipher,
Each symbol is illegible and beyond perception.
It's as though my own mind is conspiring against me
And continually torturing with a cruel deception.

The Love Lost

It started out great, happy memories we shared,
You didn't need tell us, we knew that you cared.

Maybe even a role model, inspiring to me.
You helped us to learn and provided life's key.

So, what changed? Why now the lull?
Once it was brilliant so why was our love culled?

False, empty promises meld into the lies,
As angry retorts start to blinker my eyes.

No-one is expecting a thriving rapport,
But it seems that to you even talking's a chore.

It saddens to think that you're sat there alone,
And yet even still you can't pick up the phone.

I can't quite see anymore, don't know who you are,
No matter what you say, your cares seem so far.

Your daughter is there, why can't you see,
The perfect example of what a person can be?

I know you regret and I know that you're proud,
So please bring back hope and remove this shroud.

The Vortex

Black peaks rocking, heaving; the creaking of oak.
Breeze captured by a cloak suspended on hooks.
Pivotal rise, immune to submersion,
Nature defied by a craftsman's fine touch.

Rope slips through iron, reflected in endless depth,
Supporting our mass while oars slide through tide.
Current drags us forwards, entices our keel
Towards an unknown destination, unseen by our eyes.

A vortex of altitude, underneath our horizon.
A salt scented paradise, disturbed by a rupture.
Dark formations loom over, drowning out blue.
Light disappearing, dispersed overhead

Beyond our mortal eyes, confirming our woe.
And now it becomes evident, the curse that we face.
A break in the bows, waves broken by space.
A pit near eternal, a blackness ne'er before seen.

The portal to who-knows-where, the wormhole to the terminus.
Sound disappears, a vacuum intervenes, those oak oars feel useless
As we approach an immaterial enemy.
Row, row, row all you like, take heed of beauty while you can.

Because much like that sailboat drifting to oblivion,
We're all only here for so long.

Hollow Promise

Take it out on him, it's his duty to bear.
Take it out on him, you beautiful soul.
Take it out on him, let him relight your spark,
The things that you feel should not be faced alone.

A night splattered with actions unspeakable has passed,
And your whole mind is battered by grief.
Yet there you are drowning and choked,
How can you retain self-belief?

And you plead…

"Throw me an anchor, a life raft of hope,
Tell me I'm worth something, that you won't let me go.
I can't bear to see you slipping, your fingers seem so far.
I'm afraid and I'm helpless, another dumb hoe.

But I'm not! Can't you see that? I am yours in whole!
The things that you told me were but falsity.
I lay here alone, only horror surrounds me.
You disgust me, why have I lost your security?

I'm done with your madness, your cold fronted lies,
I'm left here to wonder who I really should,
Despise."

Sleep Paralysis

A creak on a staircase I know to be rigid,
Faint frosty fog seeps through the banister,
Shimmery fluorescence flickering.

But then I'm awake. My conscious returns
And I realise it's just my father, come to
Wish me goodnight. Turning to face me
And whispering words in a tongue I can't hear,
The face begins to twist like wax under a wick,
It begins to drip, over his lip.

As irises yellow and the bones corrode,
The sockets hollow and blackness flowed,
Cast into shadow his figure did loom,
Raised as if hooked, oppressing in gloom.

I intended to scream, rushed air to my lungs
But muted breath barricaded my salvation,
Silence ensued as the demon continued mutation.

Pupils dilated I took a fateful glance,
Back down towards my chest where my heart
Pounded and my ribcage heaved.

And like that he was gone.

Drenched in sweat I searched for my oppressor,
But once again I was a young child alone.

My movement returned, but I will never forget
The horror I felt from that evil possessor.

Ersatz Fatherhood

The bike sat proud amidst autumnal leaves,
A smiling face leant over the handlebars
With a devilish shriek, a maniac laugh.
Innocent enjoyment perspiring fun,
His eyes soaking in wisdom
One inch at a time.
Spraying water from muddy puddles
The blue frame glints sunlight
Reflecting a bright happiness.
The smell of fresh bark from a billion
Forest pines coats waxy needles
Littered across the tree roots.
I run down the hill after him,
Picking up pace as he heads to the
Stream wellingtons first, stomping
In the current, soaked to the bone,
Kicking out droplets, unfazed by
Rocks, tiny form evading blockade.
Wary sheep watch on as they observe
His wonder. Nature is his home.
It prompts an ersatz paternity,
Embellishing something in me that
I'd only ever looked up to and admired,
I never imagined it to be me. Yet my
Heart rate flourishes and directs itself
Toward him, the rhythm beats his name.
An unintended love that continues to grow.
Later, as tired eyes settle and chest
Starts to heave, I grip a small fist
And helplessly feel my lips curl
Into a loving smile.

Palpable Fear

Opening my eyes has never felt so painful,
Having everything is so hard to deal with.
I never dared imagine happiness like this,
I'm terrified what I have is unravelling myth.

I feel it climbing the nape of my neck,
A molten cloak trickling ever closer,
Seeping inside to the confines of my mind,
And threatening to eradicate closure.

I love her you see, she is everything to me,
I've never wanted anything more;

Than to walk with her,

To the moon, beyond that!

Even further!

And stare back at a world we built together.

But tonight it hurts, why I don't know.
This fear is grasping and my rationale broke.
Bring back my freedom, I am my own foe,
A weeping wasteland, scared that she'll go.

I know that I'm safe here yet I cannot rest,
Memories skate by and I smile.
You cannot hurt me, you blasphemous fiend!
With her I will conquer, your scorn is vile.

The Choice

As the car veers, instinctively I pull back the wheel,
But what if I didn't?
What if I allowed nature's forces to pull me
Ever closer to the edge?
Maybe I would teeter on the foliage covered bank,
Or maybe the wheels would grip the loose dirt
And throw me into a hopeless void.

What if I refused to steer?
I wonder if I would survive the fall.
As my mechanical residency began to tumble and flip,
Would it become my coffin or my life jacket?

What if I chose to drift off the cliff?
In a melee of dirt and wood splintered from trees that blockade me,
Would my frail limbs and organs survive?

But again I swerve back into the road,
Staying in my lane as I am taught to.
A second later, I know I chose well,
As I receive a phone call from a devoted loved-one.
Momentary doubt has abandoned my mind,
As I remember that I am adored.

Poetic Energy

At night I sit searching for verse and metaphor,
Pouring over the table, to my mind I implore.

Do I describe a soaring eagle? The beauty of sunlight?
Or should I think darker and depict a bleak political fight?

What else would please them, what do they want to hear?
How should I approach this to spread joy and cheer?

I must teach a lesson! Show people the way!
I must help to guide them, to survive the fray!

But how do I do that, these are but words,
Mere characters in a phone, it feels so absurd

To think it could aid and brighten your day,
Keep demons from crossing and hold evil at bay.

They tumble like gemstones, these endless rhymes,
I panic and flourish, time after time.

It must be perfect, beautiful and true!
"Roses are red, violets are blue"

But who really cares if these words share phonetics?
I just want them to help you feel... energetic.

The Cliff

Together we stand peering over the edge,
Our feet dangling below swinging slowly back and forth.
You knock a small rock from a ledge and it tumbles
Into the abyss, falling seemingly forever.
It's terrifying to think of what would happen if that were us,
If we were the ones slammed against the cliff face,
Tumbling helplessly, vulnerable and untethered.

But what if we leaped? Would we make it then?
If we didn't even think and threw ourselves outwards,
In a beautiful arc meeting the welcoming water below.
You grasp my hand firmly while you ponder this aloud.
Your other hand securely gripping the ground afraid to let go.
Then we stand up, and feel the breeze hit our face.
It feels even higher than we expected, our stomachs are the first to fall.

But then I feel the pull from your arm and I am inspired.
Suddenly it's too late, we are committed!
We plunge into nothing, air rushing by pulling the skin from our face.
Our very hair feels dragged from its roots and fear clasps a hand around our throats!
The surface grows closer, the way the sun gleams across the bow of waves is so welcoming.
But it's so far away! Our legs are surely going to break.
Yet then we've made it. The cold gush of a whole ocean surrounds us, it's so fulfilling.
The only question that remains is, why did we even think at all?

Midnight

Upon that first chime I jolted awake,
Emerging from a stupor that fatigue imposed.

I turned to my side to find your diamond eyes
And by the second chime I was locked to them,
Hypnotized as though by a pendulum swing,
Willingly trapped in a devoting gaze.

As I reached to pull you closer,
Placing my chin upon your collarbone,
I felt a warm pulse within your throat;
Each beat dulled fear, heightened desire.

By the third chime concern was vanquished,
I was calm, dragged from a nightmare hell
And led down a path lit by your smile.

Upon the fourth stroke I brushed my lips
Across your neck and held them there
While the clock continued to strike.

Twelve times it rang for you,
My midnight sanctuary,
With every tick, I fall more in love with you.

Inspiration

The Inspiration

While we walk around blind lost in what we see,
With eyes closed you think and dreams come in a spree.

Inspire me with your philosophical view,
I want to be part of this rational crew.

Wormholes and aliens take up your mind,
While considering dimensions and what we could find,

If we just opened up and looked past what we know,
We could learn harmony and begin to grow.

Words take form and your soul paints shapes,
Constantly searching for meaningful escapes.

You'll never be alone with a mindset like yours,
You know that I'll follow, with a round of applause.

Thought Droplets

Sometimes I feel as though language drives itself.
That I am merely a foot on a pedal, pushing forwards
Along roads already paved out before me.

The curves are so elegant, the straights stretch for miles,
And my poems are the track marks,
Laid out in the rear-view mirror.

Metamorphosis

It came all at once on a literate cue,
Striding through darkness and taking a pew.

Firmly fixated on transforming my life,
A friendship with meaning where promise was rife.

A new-found belief in love and in trust,
I never imagined a relationship so just.

Platonic in nature but widening my views,
To particle physics and becoming my muse.

Don't ever forget what you mean to this man,
With a hopeless mind who knows now he can.

You know you're important and that you are great.
You're more than just that, you're my altered state.

A Hero

Cast us a shadow with your inspiring wings.
Show us a pathway and the joy that life brings.

"Help us!" We scream as all hope leaves our chest,
Again and again our fears are suppressed…

…just the way you professed.

Neither our God or our Christ or a saviour may you be,
Yet still you're a hero and ensure we feel free.

"Thank you!" we scream from the bottom of our heart,
I don't ever, ever want to see us apart.

The Dancer

As one with the rhythm, flowing like a ribbon,
I watch as you navigate the stage.
With your head risen, bursting with reason,
I'm drawn to the pleasure you wage.

In sonic alignment, a thriving assignment,
Your form is as elegant as silk.
A strong advertisement for perfect refinement,
Flaunting a skill of the highest ilk.

Strutting on a platform that you adorn,
Blurred lighting accentuates class.
I admire your life form as you perform,
As delicate as freshly blown glass.

Binary Love

A digital presence with a beating heart.
We love what we cannot see,
Loyal to a binary string of endless algorithmic alliances.
Seeing, feeling, but never perceived or tangible.

A screen is our medium,
A paranormal glimpse at what could be.
  Yet we flourish,
    Lost,
      Found,
Drawn away from what we are told is real we find true accord.

Hell

As lamplight looks on bringing rooms into focus,
Often we think of the things that near broke us.
Terror filled memories spin round in a flurry
And eyes widen bright sprung to action with worry.

But most could not even try to comprehend,
The things that I feel as I envisage my end.
An end that's not nigh but could well have been scribed,
You placed down my pen and ensured I survived.

I ponder the days where I quivered afraid,
Desperate and empty, my tattered soul frayed.
Blinded by hate of a world I can't stand,
I realise a new future, one you could see planned.

It took me a second, a month or a week,
Who knows why you tried but my outlook was bleak.
You cared more than any and to you I must tell,
Thank you, my Mother, for curing my hell.

Starbucks

A close encounter of the briefest kind,
Enough to remind and satisfy the mind.

You stood there in line awaiting coffee again,
Hearing nothing but 'Latte for Helen!' Times ten.

Then finally seated, normality resumed,
Thought after thought and stories consumed.

Sitting there swimming in roasted perfection,
Watching conversation flow in every direction.

Proud of each other, needing of the same,
It doesn't take long before I'm glad that I came.

The definition of friendship personified right there,
Beaming right back from the opposite chair.

Your choice in beverage may well be controversial,
But your kindness and wit are forever inertial.

Anger

Demonic Possession

Malevolent prevalence with occult demeanor,
Exorcised sickness, sent back to the pit.
You're shackled and chained, as I once was,
I pray that you pay for the crimes you commit.

When I close my eyes, blackened irises stare back.
Yellow embers bleed from my skin,
Where you left traces of sulphur in my capillaries,
A lasting reminder of unearthly possession.

Slashed down by holy water, cast aside to fire,
Your evil continues but in another domain.
So far removed from love, I pity your soul,
As you suffer an eternity drowned in hellish rain.

Unforgotten Enemy

I've ripped you limb from limb in my mind,
Crushed your bones in my fist.

I've torn the skin from your ribcage,
To reveal a heart so blackened and scarred.

I've screamed your name from the rooftops,
As a warning for everyone to heed.

A vein of rot in an affluent life,
You'll never be more than flawed.

Unbroken

I break my skin with conviction,
The way that you splintered my hope.
My focus is steadily slipping,
I'm searching for a noose in the rope.

Leave me to freeze in my misery,
While your conscience remains intact.
I can't cope with your lack of compassion,
As my insides begin to contract.

I remember feeling sick from the pain,
It spewed from within like the hate
I have for each fibre of your being.
I can't help needing to medicate.

But I'm broken, not beaten,
And I know I'll bounce back.
You will not defeat me!
I can stand through any attack.

You miserable soul, why are you this way?
Are you really so desperate and weak?
That you must abuse and deceive,
And twist any chance that you seek?

I'm better than that, just you watch,
While I climb up out of this abyss.
I'll show you what my life can be,
And unleash a magnificent bliss.

Stranded

Lost in a ruthless wilderness, panic spreads quick.
Like spiders infest, it envelops and strives,
To threaten, ingest and then take fight,
Against very morale, more than ever it thrives.

Be a source of hydration in the desert,
We are but barren wasteland devoid of a soul.
Be a lifesaving spring in an otherwise barren landscape,
As we bellow for aid while our journey takes toll.

Nightlife rife with detestable folk.
Politicians petition for darker days.
Anguish extinguished then rekindled again.
Brutality and inequality continue to have their say.

Our world is devoid of logic and sense,
The drought less and less metaphorical.
Imagine someday that you'll quench our thirst,
But right now, so bleak is the oracle.

Sand fills our eyes, so stranded are we,
Unseeing and lost without destination.
Is it useless to search for an exit?
When we know that we are a doomed nation?

Love

Aortic Mansion

My veins are the pathways on which you make your daily commute, leading up to the ventricle door. Kicking your shoes in the atrium porch, a faint flickering fire crackles clumsily from an obscured room, forming dancing shadows on the walls.

From the outside I see dim light from gas lanterns shine through the crooked frames of windows haphazardly cut through the tissue. From here I watch as you make my heart home, beneath the shingle roof tiles where an aorta chimney pushes plumes of your faithful smoke outwards.

Inside there is crumbled paintwork set against rotting wood, drawing the eye to where you sit hunched over an old oak study desk, pouring over books from a towering bookcase. Those shelves are a Dewey Decimal key to my mind and you desperately seek the answer to every issue I tackle.

My chest is your mansion and you are always at home. If I heave the brass knocker on the dense wooden door I know you will answer, my hospitable reprieve.

Snowed In

While the storm outside bangs at my door,
And pledges to wage outright war,
Cutting me off from the world around,
Ripping at roof tiles with an awful sound,
I worry not for all that I require
Is to sit inside and relax by the fire.

Surrounded by people I love with full heart,
From here I have no need at all to depart.

A Letter To A Lover

Ah memories, those wonderful little electrical charges
So innocently pulsing through our brains, dancing incredible,

Defying all logic, making us feel like absolute crap.
Such a beautiful concept, the mind. Scientifically speaking it's a marvel.

The fact that we can *think*. Who would have thought it?
But my God is it flawed! Why can't something so beautiful be elegant?

Why did our 'creator' allow such an obvious chink in our armour?
Call it user error, call it whatever the hell you want but it's a crying shame.

At night is the worst, like the day has burned it out and it can
Only cycle through the shit buried deep within its rusty cogs.

I was happy this morning. What happened?
Why can I now only see darkness and fear?

Fear and darkness, darkness and fear.
Fear and darkness, darkness and fear.

Such a gift we were given to be human, we have been gifted
An unrivalled intelligence, an ability to imagine.

Imagine…

We can appreciate beauty, benefit from natures perfection.

We can achieve, build, grow and improve. How lucky are we.

We're all so lucky.

So why can I only picture my feet on ledges?

Why do loving smiles fade from my 'incredible' mind?

Like they are just vapour, vaporising?
Is it just me? Where did I go wrong?

Don't get me wrong I adore music, melody soothes me, helps, guides, saves me.
I see that I am loved, surrounded by joy, I give thanks for that.

Like you I am lucky, I couldn't ask for more.
I don't need to! I am happy, life is good to me.

But it doesn't stop me hurting, when that pesky mind acts up.
Like a trying toddler, pushing his luck.

Tell me it isn't just me that feels this way.
That you hurt the same way I do, that you don't understand either.

I've learned to welcome the pain, to profit from its steady flow.
To allow it to consume me and test my defences.

Because let's be honest. If I didn't hurt, how could you make me feel
So great over and over again?

The Bridge

I will never forget that evening by the bridge.
While we stood there attempting to salvage

A way of committing, of finding a way.
I'll never regret the choice I made that day.

In a life-changing year, a moment changed my life.
Surrounded by nothing but ourselves and wildlife

I saw my future clearer than I ever knew
It was possible to feel, a knowledge so true.

Half caste trees, abandoned by the sunset's incandescence,
We walked hand in hand while dusk fell less and less luminous.

Surrendering sunlight danced upon the surface of water,
A scene so new to me, but one you often thought of.

Pieces never aligned so snugly side by side
As when those thoughts and ambitions flowed like a tide.

Strolling down a pathway in mind and in matter,
Watching with wonderment as shadows did scatter.

A world of opportunity rearing its head,
Yet transatlantic freedom only fills me with dread.

With such a decision to make, it seemed there was none,
Anything other than this would surely be wrong.

My…

Deserving of adoration, you stand proud and true,
Beaming with grace as you look upon me.
The smell of fresh coffee drifts in the atmosphere while we talk,
Aimlessly and effortlessly recounting our lives.

The appealing aroma leads me to wonder how you do the same…

You wear the same perfume as a million others,
Yet your scent is so distinct.
Like a rose without thorns or a crackling fire without the choking smoke.

You don't see what I see…

As if you're peering through a kaleidoscope and observing a mere refraction.

Oh, everything at once, hurtling forwards,
Forwards,
Constantly,
Forwards.

And yet we remain static, refusing to be derailed,
Our hands interlocked and our hopes in line.
Endlessly,
Always,
Endlessly,

Whilst curing my fever with your medicinal prose,
Remember you're worth more than you'll ever know.

That Eye Thing

Pull me in, kiss me, whisper in my ear,
Spill feeling from your irises, speak low to me.
Allow me to reap an undying novelty,
Ameliorated, content, an omnipotent amour.

Pheromone glance, locked into place,
As if eyes are connected by wires, a positively charged
Electrical muse galvanizing fulfilment,
All the while eradicating aversion.

Our world exists in a metre square, the rest but a blur,
A figment, a parallel universe teeming with nothing
That matters, nothing worth even considering.
For I am you and you are I, we are we.

For a second, a minute, a month – who knows?
We stay there eyes locked then you whisper,
Syllables never meant so much to a man
As when you whisper, "Babe, I adore you."

Queen

It's amazing to see just what I can achieve,
When I cross all my boundaries and uncover my tongue.
The details come slipping and fall through my teeth,
My answers to questions that rendered me numb.

How can the virtue of speech be so pure?
And harness such power as words start to strut?
I was locked in a prison with bars made of wood,
You gave me a hacksaw and I started to cut.

This happiness surely can't be more than a dream.
But each morning I wake up and still see your form.
A shadowy figment of someone else's imagination,
I am the lucky one, able to feel your warmth.

Laid by your side with your arm pulled across me,
I fumble for closeness and sense your feelings spout.
You make me feel regal and you gave to me a crown
Made from rose bush with all the thorns pulled out.

Understanding Love

As I lay there with my head against your pulse,
And your fingers gently flicking through my hair,
I begin to wish that I could see through that skull,
And examine the thoughts that reside under there.

Your mind is a soul portal that offers no passage.
Your eyes are the windows with the curtains pulled closed.
But as I swim in their depth, I begin to care not,
For I see your eternal love for me enclosed.

The silvery moonlight washes over your face,
You become a metallic jewel in surrounding black.
I take in its beauty like water from a well,
As I run my hand along your alluring back.

Love is imperfect and gives birth to doubt,
But as much as my consciousness attempts to cripple me,
I will push through the pain and find the azure,
That indigo solace that renders me free.

Observations Of The World Around Me

The Moor

Whilst crossing the deepest secret of Yorkshire's moors,
I find myself forced to stop and to pause.
The setting before me is anything but bland,
I find myself travelling an ovine ruled land.

Wildlife is everywhere, it's as though they are allied,
Sheep cling to the slopes of a heather-strewn hillside.
A kestrel soars, eyes strafing its prey,
While rabbits cease lunging, barbed fence in their way.

The biting breeze blows at my ears,
Picking up pace and going through the gears.
It pushes slight waves towards the boathouse,
And rustles through leaves as quiet as a mouse.

I stare into wilderness, leant into your arms,
Hedge lines lead out towards revolving wind farms.
Atop the bridge we look down on the valley,
The tall pine tops swing like a mast o'er a galley.

Soft powdered snow lies next to the bank,
Gradually spreading out onto the gangplank.
Tree roots emerge like serpents in an ocean,
Twisting and writhing without any motion.

Sparse scattered houses lay sporadically strewn,
Under a castle left crumbling to ruin.
A tulip grows lonely within the thicket,
Wrapped delicately around a wooden fence picket.

45 Rockefeller Plaza

As I stand and stare upward the earth starts to fall,
It cascades around me but never touches down.
The buildings plunge as cirrus races by,
Dynamic in form like a sinuous gown.

Eyes back to the horizon, between the municipal valley,
I'm drawn there by roads formed as parallel lines.
Endless by design they dip as they swell,
Flowing through the city like fine flowing wines.

The elevator climbs and I feel the suspense,
A veritable dream is about to come true,
But I could never explain the awe from the top,
That kind of shock needs a first-person view.

A God amongst mortals I stand and observe,
An endless array of urban relief.
From here I see colours I didn't even know existed
And a paradox of life on this island of reef.

Skyscrapers are caught in the crossfire
Of blinking stars that shine from above.
I raise my arms up towards the moon,
And watch over this city that I've come to love.

Old Oak

Are you alive, O wizened oak?
With your branches withered,
Spread out like wicker
Surviving the blizzard,
Are you a wizard?
You seem to have it figured,
Casting spells as
Your boughs flicker.
Though the weather is bitter
You stood the time test,
Like a lizard
Replenishing its tail.
Year after year
Your leaves littered,
Despite the weather shiver
Your roots still slither
And you stand as a pillar
To the ground tethered.

Whitby Harbour

The sound of clanging bells chimes through the breeze,
Jostling in aerial battle with the cries of native gulls.
The gently heaving yachts climb and then fall
As the water in the harbour rises and then lulls.

I stand by the jetty and take in the smell
Of an ocean so endless, beyond that high wall.
The aroma is carried by a crisp coastal breeze,
In the distance I see tankers and fishermen trawl.

Nearer to me those sailboats foreshadow a town,
Antiquated and picturesque, a jewel placed on a map.
Historical stonework leads around the jetty
Against which cascades of gentle waves slap.

The town's crown is the abbey, elegant and bold,
Perched on a hillside with steeple intact.
The steps seem like ribbon as they lead to its door,
Winding a way towards a cultural artefact.

As my eyes skirt up, tracing the mast of an old naval ship
Towering over all other vessels,
I hear the small flags flap vigorously in the wind
And the groans from its moorings with which it wrestles.

Sunshine glares on and although it is cold,
This scene warms the senses and brightens the day.
In the moment, I wonder and ponder aloud.
Who would want anything but to experience this bay?

The Canal

I'm sat by a canal as the cyclist passes.
A scene so fabricated but natural in nature.

The water flows closer to the bridge, easing a way
Downstream toward the bustle of life.

The road, a concrete arc gracefully crossing
The path laid for swans, an aquatic ribbon.

A small dog is next to pass, tail wagging, mind a whirl
Overloaded with scent, scenery, opportunity.

Still the water flows and I realise how constant it is.
Nothing changes for my presence. I am here

But no one knows; I serve no purpose in this intricate scene.
I am no greater than the birds in the trees,

The creaking of boughs, the dancing of boats teasing their moorings.
I am but matter in this universe, I'm far from its core.

A peripheral proton, an unperceivable entity.
I feel only humbled by what I have seen,

By how much is contained in such a simple scene.
And ideas tumble like the canal through the lock,

We could all realise what we have, if we only took stock.

Humber

Don't you find it amazing the way a tide is constant?
Perpetually flowing without stopping to repose.
I watch it drag silt and sediment before me,
While sunlight bounces from the crests of gravity fed waves.

An oystercatcher pulls tediously at the muddy bank,
As stubborn and determined as the river itself,
Constantly hoping to uncover its prey;
That beneath ooze and sand lies a prize of nutrition.

I follow its path as it begins to take flight,
Its wings soaring fluently on the current.
Then it hangs in the air as if tied to a string,
A puppet held aloft held by unseen hands.

It is framed in the structure of a mighty bridge
Which spans the river, elegant as a tight-rope.
An engineering marvel, artificial phenomenon,
It rules over all like a monarch on a throne.

It's towers like sceptres and ropes like a leash,
It holds onto nature with a sturdy hand.
Surely defying science as it stretches beyond sight,
Into the mist and far distant lands.

Tide may flow beneath, but it's purpose remains true,
Holding traffic aloft and allowing safe passage,
Nothing can stop such a human born godsend,
A concrete tribute to immaculate resolve.

The View

From here bustling life is invisible to me,
Snow quilted slopes stretch as far as I see.

A breeze blows on by that no-one else can feel,
Delicate like waves on a lonely ship's keel.

To look down from here upon everything is strange,
My own elevated pew on top of the range,

With my feet firmly planted I feel orchestic,
And see what the world really is, majestic.

Glistening light from a million window panes,
It feels like someone released constricting chains.

I'm freezing cold, yet my marvel commences,
Smoke from a thousand fires warms my senses.

They don't see what I see, only their own mundane chores,
They know not of being watched by someone who adores

Each chimney like pinpricks, each car a grain of sand,
Distant yet close over acres of land.

My mind meanders freely like the river passing the mill,
Silky and flowing like ink from a quill.

It's lonely up here, all I can do is ponder,
What a beautiful world we have, it's so full of wonder.

Countryside

Crumbling brickwork below
  Tumbling tiles.
    Fumbling ivy around a
      Grumbling gateway.
        Rumbling iron beside a
          Mumbling drainpipe.
            Humbling hearth made from
              Stumbling stones.

Beating sunshine with
  Fleeting fog.
    Greeting wind chill shifting
      Retreating rain clouds.
        Sheeting ice,
          Seating sown seeds.
            Tweeting bluebird and
              Bleating black sheep.

Snoring livestock and
  Soaring swallows.
    Enduring crops cut by
      Choring combines.
        Alluring grassland grazed by
          Adoring animals.
            Pouring milk pales beside a
              Roaring riverside.

A Single Willow

Standing there, boughs askew, immovable mass.
Growing invisibly, time tells tales of your prominence;

Of your creaking inflection, your stance on the slope
Of a grain carpeted wasteland, a bed for your roots.

Solitary confinement, yet plain for all to see,
Incapable of movement without the aid of wind.

As I stare you catch rays and disperse them like fans.
A photosynthetic miracle, casting oily green hue.

Set against nothing, a perpetual sky
We see but a fraction of your grandiose anatomy.

Gnarly knuckles held aloft you're in a constant position of prayer,
Sprouted from dirt, a colossal beast personified by a seed.

Unseen anchors spread beneath our very feet
Holding you strong while you contort with grace,

Uncalculated yet majestic, an innate artistry.
Your lack of companionship draws nought but attention

To the elegance and illustriousness your limbs possess.
Stand there eternal, sempiternal Goddess.

Weather And Seasons

Winter Storm

Drifted snow surmounts the pavements,
Powdery residue from a since passed storm.
It's white shining brilliance reflects the sun,
In perfect contrast against radiant blue.

Razor-sharp icicles dangle like stalagmites.
…Or are they stalactites, I'm unsure.
Regardless, they're hung in a balance,
Impossibly clinging to every ledge.

Shadows in tandem with the bitter wind,
Pulled across the ice as clouds pass by.
Each of them precipitate be it gradual or swift,
Casting frost-bitten earth into further strain.

Winter Sun

Razor edged disc your light is still pale,
Weaker than it will be in a month or two.
Your arc still peaks low in an unblemished sky,
In blinding angelic glare; casting majestic hue.

As I stare it's as though your circumference revolves,
I know I shouldn't look but I'm hooked like a moth.
Wintery mornings provide solace and bliss, I
Wallow in a new-found purity, like a man of the cloth.

You project long shadows, as drawn out as the night,
Exaggerating the beauty of every tree branch,
Of a weather vane caught in your path;
Cockerel silhouette strewn over ground you blanch.

Oh, razor edged disc, you enlighten this world,
But where do you go when the horizon submerges you?
Luckily for us when you abscond and evoke night,
We find equal beauty in indigo blue.

The Frost

As frost latches grip onto human built structures
And cloaks each detail with a crystalline caress,
Its feathery skeleton scintillates brightly,
And flows over terrain like a white bridal dress.

Skating on water and grasping at leaves, nothing escapes
Its mighty autocracy, it's scything oppression.
Perilous it may be, threatening our wellbeing,
But we admire its glisten, its detailed composition.

It aids moonlight's dance and ameliorates sunlight
While it glows as a warning that we must heed.
A sure sign of winter carved into the ice,
And blossoming cold proving autumn did concede.

First Sign Of Spring

It happened today at last! Finally!
The moment I've been waiting for.
It finally happened, after so long!
But happening all the same, finally! At last!

Winter's execution, laid out on the guillotine,
Where a warm sultriness cuts through it's neck,
Giving way to Spring's cunning regime.
I felt it today, finally! I've waited so long!

Frost dispersed by sunshine, at last!
The cold breeze punctuated by warmth.
The first signs of change flickering by,
I felt it brush across my back.

Feeling In Nature

Floral Decay

Cut down in the prime of life you sit there spent,
Destined to brighten a home, to be on display.
Your stems and your petals were a romantic gift,
Given with love on Cupid's own day.

As the focal point of the living room,
The roses serve purpose with reddish enrichment,
But the lilies lay dormant, unopened and plain,
Incapable of marvel, lacking bewitchment.

The leaves start to curl as assured death takes toll,
Their brownish blades remain cupped and bear rust.
Yet there is a strange beauty to their failed growth,
Semi-opened, even near their end their attempt to thrust.

Surely we all should watch on and take note,
That beside perfection, these lilies still refuse
To give up, to admit defeat, and they succeed!
A clear minority – unworthy to most becomes my muse.

Like Bardo

As hands on a clock reset, so does the sun.
When the day glow vanishes and leaves you behind,
Do not fear,
For you can still bathe in the moonlight.

Life is a cyclical beauty and what lies between
The sun's rise and fall can be equally radiant.
The night is like bardo, a temporary death.
Bridging the gap between one life and the next.

We must learn that patience is an essential trait,
For tomorrow will arrive as a second chance conceived.
At dawn you can stand in the mountains and bathe
In the deep orange glow,

Reincarnated,
As whatever you make of yourself.

Reborn,
As your own greatest dream.

The Storm

I: The Peace
Drift with me darling in an idyllic paragon.
Swim in the ether, breathe in its elixir.
Combine your very membrane with the oceanic swell.
Organic like the crests, innate we forget.

II: The Approach
Ears prick up, audible vibration, a vibrato reverb.
The scent on your very tongue, it's alive, it creeps near.
Gloom pierced with a strobe, or is it a blade?
A visual clap, brightens your awe.

III: The Swell
Hostile Demi-God attempting a coo,
Spinning our Earth, bending the physics, melding sea and sky.
It hits like our terror, sudden… immediate.
Ethereal razor blades dispersing, dragging us, ending us for sure.

IV: The Passing
And it's extinguished. The way it began. The cackle of wildlife resumes,
Mocking our panic. Bend your ear to the distant roar,
The inkwell of torment on our horizon.
Another person's burden to weather.

V: The Calm
Cheer loud, for what subdued us taught us.
Let birdsong prevail, allow yourself laughter.
The waves now lap gentle and provoke us to dwell,
We held onto what mattered, together we're calm.

Urban Flourish

How beautiful are the city lights?
I stare through diamond eyes,
Place teeth against teeth as my tongue feels tied.
My ears prick up as a siren cries.

Lamplight falls as fluorescent fog.
Obliterating nature with a luminous hue.
A sense of awe drowns my senses,
I am a leaf engulfed by a tirade of dew.

As a knife cuts through rope,
Your ghost drifts through space.
Humanity's creation laid out right there,
This sensation is hard to displace.

Walk with me through acres of substance
And find yourself within the glow
Of a thousand million thoughts and ideas,
A flourishing urban meadow.

Let those naive diamond eyes be inspired
By a torrent of cultural matter.
Imagine yourself exceptional,
Allow your limitations to shatter.

Imaginings

Untitled

We've been sat here so long that the windows have started
To fog. I use the side of my palm to scrape away moisture,
So we can continue to appreciate the endless valley below.
What's the first thing you hear when you open the door, the peacefully
oppressive silence or the lethargic hum of an
insect's wings beating out of view?

Take in the iridescent landscape, skimmed by shadow as
Clouds beat by, swallowing sunlight then restoring its glow;
It touches everything, that lustrous glimmer. Each of the trees
In that coniferous woodland are drenched in it and in the breeze
We can hear their creak.

We trace our eyes down an old picket fence line, which time has led
To decay; knotted eyes stare back with a mutual respect, for we're
Part of the same calm rural scene. As we lay out our blanket and
Uncork the wine, the gratifying heat licks our backs; summer is nigh
And for today and today only, this rolling hillside is but ours.

Inky Black

Somewhere out there in the deep fathoms of space,
An asteroid throws itself through an uninhabitable void.
Planets pivot on their axis and stars explode as supernova
Seen a hundred centuries later, suspended and forsaken.

Earthly units of measurement become so insignificant,
We speak in lightyears to describe places we'll never see.
Celestial shipwrecks, a spatial silhouette,
A backdrop eternal, through which our world streams.

Gaseous gargantuan sits like a bottle top on the horizon,
While icy cold rings encircle its enormous mass,
Shadowed by the moons that orbit it like offspring
And spin an incessant masquerade, magnificent to the end.

From our pale blue dot, we witness eternity
Perpetually passing before our eyes.
That faint twinkling is a whole galaxy! and we'll never know
What it contains within its rim.

As comet tails streak and the sun rises and sets
Like clockwork, our planet continues to gyrate.
A gesture perfected over four billion years,
To be repeated for four billion after we're gone.

Sunset

Trembling island, teetering on the edge of night.
A half-light, casting no shadow but dancing with colour.
Alive like a planetary firefly, the scale of sky knows no bounds.
A halo of orange blends into dusky black

As a peaceful mirage turns like clockwork toward me.
Faint twinkling stars spread nearer the horizon
Whilst surrendering birdsong grows faint.
Like the commuting traffic behind me they dim their voices,

Seek rest after another uplifting and fruitful day.
A day that brought a brisk freshness, relief from winter,
Cold and crisp yet irrefutably beautiful,
Reminiscent of a long since passed summer.

Spring time approaches, like the airplane overhead
That catches rays from an already set sun
And reflects them from its metallic shell.
I wonder where it is headed? It is homebound

Or destined for somewhere far flung
As it disappears into darkness, only a mere fragment
Of this magnificent moment. Time and space embodied
By physical interpretation, passing before me.

As dusk becomes night I close my eyes to think
Of the reason I'm alive. It's for times like this.

Political Musings

The Moral Of The Story

Don't get me wrong I am not a religious man, far from it.
But there is something serenely beautiful about a church.
Stained glass sanctuary, sealing off an outside world of
Despair and grief.

Take a pew my friend and think on your wrongs. Place
Your hands together, scream, cry, laugh, who cares, just
Feel love and spread it amongst your compatriots. Your
Fellow sinners, your earthly comrades who suffer the same way
You do.

I watched the news this morning. Another killer, fleeing justice and
Abusing a fucked-up amendment. The thrice weekly example of
Human atrocity, just try and tell me who is watching over *that*.

Maybe I'm more religious than I think, for at least I have morals and
Know right from wrong. I may not pray to the same God that you do;
My deity is in my head but it allows me to tackle my own
Inner demons and see the world clear. That's all I need. Your God is
Fictitious anyway, right? And that's ok too.

Who cares where we came from or why we are here, let's save
That question for another day. First and foremost, shouldn't we
Be asking who we really are? Why do we hurt each other and why
Do we blame? Why is the power of empathy so much weaker than
The power of an AR-15?

If we can't answer those questions, then maybe we shouldn't even
Be here at all.

Humandroid

March with me baby, to the beat of this drum.
March to the drum, the beat of this drum.
Listen to that drumbeat and march to its rhythm,
That drumbeat you hear renders your mind numb.

A military cue with an Orwellian tune…

Listen to me baby, follow my voice,
My voice is right here, my bellowing voice.
Listen to my voice as I tell you your wrongs,
Right here, I'm screaming, my voice is but noise!

A symbol of pleasure, of comfort and pain,
Painful distraction, distracting your dreams.
Focus on me, lay your eyes there, over here
Toward me and my eloquent themes.

I WILL guide you,

I WILL show you,

Teach you. Like it or not I will teach you.
Teach you to live, to survive and die,
Die knowing that you have me by your side.
Aside from that know there is no respite.

'Coz this is life you see, we're lost from the start,
Lost while we're guided, guided apart.
Apart from each other we know not ourselves, a part of us can't.

Can you?

I'll leave you to ponder your own self-belief,

Ponder it, wonder it, make your thoughts brief.
March to the beat of this drum as you think,
The drumbeat gets louder, march to it in sync.

Closed Circuit TV Stars

I see you up there, I can see that you see me.
The little red blink gives away your presence.
I listen to you drone about our right to freedom,
About the way you will fight for our national security

While overhead, drones watch, intrude. Conspire?
Lift the lid on our rights as you peer through the crack
And expose what we are, but for what?
To what end? What did we do wrong?

Don't get me wrong I'm an intelligent man,
I can see both sides, in a way I feel safe.
I feel comforted by your presence, protected by it.
Threatened by it, like everyone else.

Flawed legislation and snooper's charters,
Lack of scrutiny and parliamentary negligence
Leave us to wonder what you really can see,
While we forget that you're there, gazing into the looking glass.

Looking,
Watching,
Always looking,
Always watching.

You are not above the law good sirs! Don't forget that
Whilst you are pushing the boundaries of our freedoms!
Even as I speak an advert appears for a website I visited three days ago.
Hint hint, it speaks of the irony that we aren't so smart,

While we trust in 'smart' TVs and 'smart' phones that harvest
Our lives and flog them to the highest bidder.

I feel exposed. Naked and cold in the street when I think
That you robbed me. Not of possession but of freedom.

Of my free will, my right to map my own course
And take comfort in the fact that I am me and me alone.
Yes I feel safe, yes you do good but alas! Don't think I forgive you.
Who would have known it, Orwell was right.

What-about-ism

What about the man who sits home and prays?
Bent to his knees, he'll never have his say.
What about forgiveness, does that even exist?
It seems juxtaposed against lies that they twist.

What about those who take from our government,
Provided for, smug, in a state of contentment.
What about profit and corporate greed?
Decades of silent oppression, yet still we don't heed.

It's their fault for exploiting capitalism!
They warp our clay minds like light through a prism!
Supposedly bettering our artificial lives,
While greater their social immunity thrives.

"It's your fault" they retort, with an authoritative voice,
"You don't work hard enough, failure is your choice."
So we must be to blame for society's crash,
Otherwise why would they be so sombre and brash?

What about conspiracy, we know we are deceived,
Sometimes I wonder how we even believed.
"What if you're wrong, do you even have proof,
That these atrocities were fabricated, that they were spoof?"

What about the fact that we only complain?
Glued to devices as we digitize our brains.
What about the shadow that sweeps overhead,
Cast by our ignorance, our self-inflicted dread.

What if we chose to pursue what we love,
We all have weaknesses we could dispose of.
What if we knew this and acted instead,

Of wallowing in pity down a path we feel led.

Fight for your freedom and fight for your cause,
But before you do so take a second to pause.
What if your solution only worsens our plight?
What if you, all-knowing, aren't completely right.

The Wall

Sometimes I wonder who really does rule,
The people or parliament or a corporate mule.
Cursed, feeling nought but dismay and betrayed,
I watch a world pass by corrupted by hate.

Closing off borders right now may suffice
To quell a small problem, put issues on ice.
But come now be logical, do you really think
That fighting blindfolded is stronger than ink?

Walls and waters might keep them at bay,
But woe betide you hear what they have to say.
It seems you've forgotten it isn't just us,
Other people's problems aren't superfluous.

The age-old adage tells that we're all the same,
But that's not quite true, we don't all bear the blame.
Just you and your power, cowardly and smug,
Making false promises then pulling the plug.

Just listen, I plead, can't you see you've become
Deaf to our prayers, only caring for income?
I can't bear to look, common sense won't prevail,
We're headed for a future where this planet will fail.

The Model Citizen

You are one of us and we are all the same,
Consigned a number and bred to be tame.
Perfect and sculpted and stood in a queue,
Understanding of order and always in view.

Conformity is the name of a game you can't win,
A nation divided in an endless tailspin.
Follow in footsteps laid out in the sand,
And walk round in circles while holding their hand.

It's pointless to question there's anything more,
Their 'wisdom' instils you right through to your core.
Life is a map, with guidance laid out,
You are but a cog, contributing to drought.

Day after day you slave and you grind,
Cursing the fact that you're part of mankind.
Look down at your feet and ignore the sky,
They laugh while they watch you struggle from on high.

You know that it's wrong, that there are other ways,
So why not bite back, set the planet ablaze.
Tear down their structure and set it alight,
Unleash your potential, stand up and fight!

Social Outlook

Antisocial Media

Bunny rabbit facelift and falsely white teeth.
Thin rimmed spectacles frame dainty freckled face.

Fluorescence the enemy blocking natural born light,
Casting fabricated shadow on pristine visage.

Cheek bone field day, brows are on point,
Emoji strewn self-portrait, digitally obtained.

Always that handsome, you'd have us all think,
Habitual lavishness, commonplace indulgence.

Hashtags scream privilege, to mask a mind that screams help,
Diverting suspicion with a brainstormed smile.

Some people use platforms as a way to stand tall.
Dispersing good feeling and positive message.

Some people use platforms as a way to stand out,
Expending of others, they spread social rot.

Body-Posi motivation side lined by merciless trolls.
Keyboard tapping dickheads worth less than their phony accounts.

Welcome to the real world, where nothing is as it seems,
These trolls and 'beauty queens' come into real focus.

Warts and all bared we see their true colours,
Just another example of internet façade.

Air Trav-Hell

Confine me to a metallic cylindrical hell,
Excrete a concoction of manufactured air.
Strapped into what must surely be made from concrete,
I bow my head and formulate mental prayer.

Being held hostage by choice
Is justified by the thought of a blissful destination,
Stockholm Syndrome sets in as I place my forehead
Against the cool glass; underneath lies another passing nation.

This isn't so bad, from here the earth is so calm,
A carpet of mountainside which rivers intertwine.
Capillary lifelines, twisting through outcrops,
A physical miracle, a creator's own shrine.

To be restricted yet free is such a strange feeling,
Hurtling through the stratosphere with the grace of an acrobat.
Uplifted yet anxious as you watch the wing flexing,
Close eyes and hope that it's supposed to do that!

Take me back to the terminal, so I can feel ground beneath my feet!
As I feel the loss in altitude my head begins to swim,
My heart pounds audibly as I clutch for support, I swear
I could touch those rooftops over which we skim.

In an instant we're down and buildings rush by,
As the blur recedes my adrenaline stops spinning.
Withdrawal kicks in, that was so incredible!
Unbelievable, an experience to fulfilling.

Oh, Society

As the Earth was passed down to us, so was its evil,
Hand-me-down grief, poverty and war.
Our forefathers battled and splattered the blood
Of enemy nations we innately deplore.

As a firefly dances with a naked lightbulb,
We flirt with the idea of living in peace.
But our cognitive development only stretches so far,
While technology advances, our morals decrease.

Forever cursed to suffer each other,
We're dying in circles, forced to live in repeat,
Where democracy makes no sense; hexed by inheritance,
We preach a love that can but retreat.

Our own lives become our panic rooms,
Where we lock out an evil truth.
Bodies stack outside the doorway like building blocks,
Forming a palace topped by a guilt-tiled roof.

Are you nervous?

Does it scare you to think that nuclear capable weapons
Sit poised on launch pads even as we speak?
That right now, people inhabit war-stricken territories,
Lose their homes and their children to havoc *our* nations wreak.

They live in a real fear, they don't have the tools to hide
Behind the same walls that we do.
And the only thing separating this from happening to us
Is the colour of our skin and the language we spew.

Think about that, think about your 'birthright'.

We should all feel sick.

Tales Of War

Waco

Immeasurable loss measured by mere statistics,
Unfathomable grief sprouted from explicit negligence.
A nimble idea sprung quick into action, calculating ingenuity,
Pushing the boundaries of concept and idea.

Glide along forwards to meet your mark,
Your worldly companions, armed to the teeth.
Each man just like you, a skin and bone construct,
Picture his flesh as it's ripped from his chest;

As a payload of lead tears a life from genealogy,
Separates him from a world that he loved.
But these men need not worry as you make your approach,
Soaring gracefully through inky black.

Your system is flawed, misjudged by a droid,
Fate is but your own, your target can breathe safe.
Horror will commence in a second or two
When you realise that you're falling short.

The beach is too far, you now see that clear,
Only icy destitution awaits.
The cold drags you in, a gale force grip surrounds
As your craft is dragged under the sea.

A visual peril twisting your reality, collapsing your lungs
And stopping your heart. Can you face it?
Can you make an escape before hope is lost?
Free your senses to free your body, pull yourself from the swell.

Your comrades are dead there is no way to save them,
The men you relied on are gone.
A simple equation confirms your jeopardy,

The shoreline is miles away.

Unimaginable cold seizes your everything!
Crippled, hopeless, forgotten, you swim.
Keep swimming, don't stop as the hours rush by.
Ignore the screams from your lungs.

The scale of death reaches an unimaginable toll,
As men meet the fathoms all around you.
Why are you here, "Fuck war!" you scream,
As an ocean invades your throat,

Left stranded by the higher power that forced you to kill
And couldn't care less if you drown.
An honest mistake they'll say, "This was a very serious disaster"
They'll be sure it won't happen again.

But it's too late for you now as the enemy sleeps on.
Unaware that you even came, at least they live on.

Operation Tiger

In a small English town backed by billowing bluffs,
A scene of serenity lay spanning the shore.
A coarse coastal bar fronting the lagoon,
Where the blue tepid tide is perfect to bathe.

Fine white sand reflects glorious sunlight,
And the greenest of fields stretch to the horizon.
Blue sky like heaven hung over the ocean
And white gulls soar free, casting shadows on the water.

As you stroll through the cove set within Lyme bay,
You'll notice an anomaly placed upon its breadth.
Carved into stone by generations past,
It tells tales of terror to which this region bore witness.

Now close your eyes and let the phantom emerge;
Imagine the clamour of calamity offshore,
Voices extinguished one hundred at a time.
Constant carnage ensuing with no hope in sight.

Operation Tiger cast into catastrophe,
As craft after landing craft suffered the same fate;
Death by drowning or death by flame,
Weighed down by life vests or dragged to the fathoms;

Bloodshed implausible yet inflicted all the same.
In your mind take a walk from the sea to the shore,
Over corpses of men abandoned by scattering ships
And take in the sound of over seven hundred screams.

Against all odds some made it to land.
But astonishingly, the order was given to continue.
Watch bullets bounce as they flick up the sand,

Thrown tirelessly from the muzzles of your countrymen's guns.

How could this happen after all you've just seen?
Now men are torn apart and bleed where they stand.
Reopen your eyes and appreciate the present,
That wasn't even battle just pointless waste of life.

Modern Warfare

Like fists in a playground the missiles rain,
Yet the only victims bear no blame.

Two days painted red that taint a whole nation.
How can we empathise with such unimaginable horror?
When we can't hear their cries or their harrowing screams?

We need not concern ourselves with what is happening
In a far-flung continent,
Our lives are already stressful enough as they are,
What with our jobs and responsibilities.
Our trauma is much greater than the mother who just saw
Her own child
Disintegrate
In front of her very eyes.

I doubt she could find the strength to walk,
Even if she hadn't been gravely disfigured.

Like fists in a playground the missiles rain,
Yet the only victims bear no blame.

A twelve-year-old lay injured, cut from head to toe.
But this isn't real to us!
This is just a mere image on a screen.
Each man is as guilty as the next of sitting by idle,
While we know the world is fucked,
We continue to attack each other
Anyway.

War crimes galore are committed with no regard,
Amnesty is but a concept in a world where

Killing
Rules over
Common sense.

Like fists in a playground the missiles rain,
Yet the only victims bear no blame.

Tear kids from their
Homes
And their
Limbs
From their corpses,

What is that laying beneath the rubble?
Destroyed within a plume of ashen smoke.
Is it the foundations of an enemy stronghold?
Or a hospital, incapacitated and unable to provide
Aid for the very people you mercilessly slaughter.

Where are the human rights?

We're all human, right?

Comical And Lighthearted Poems

To Be British For a Day

I'm sorry sir, good morning, how do you do?
Pop round after work, I'll make you a brew.

Here take my seat, I'll stand to the side.
Sorry for squeezing by, this aisle isn't wide.

The bus is late! Now I've missed my train!
Oh, not to worry, let's not cast audible blame.

Tut, how insulting, that waitress is rude!
My meal was disgusting! "Thanks for the food!"

I must approach the counter and join in the queue.
My apologies sir, you were first, "No you were!" No, you!

Oh damn, that guy is still ten seconds away!
Never mind, I'll hold open the door anyway.

Everything is going wrong; my heart just sank.
"Hi! How are you?" "I'm great thanks!"

Finally I'm home, I can flick on the TV.
Get in! Fantastic! It's fish and chips for tea!

I hope you like this poem, I really do worry,
If you don't, then you know I'm awfully sorry!

Man Flu

Unbearable pain threatens to break my morale,
A crippling ache in my ear canal.

Tell me it's justified, that I'm not just weak,
This virus is killing me, it's lasted a week!

Stop asking so much, I'm bedridden can't you see?
My cries go unanswered, a volatile plea.

I can barely move, it hurts just to think,
My migraine gets stronger every time I blink.

And still you just laugh, tell me I'm pathetic,
I'm 'making it up', my complaints are synthetic.

Man Flu you call it, what an absolute joke,
I'm genuinely ill, it's not my fault I'm a bloke!

South Circular

My fingers tap at the steering wheel,
As my tongue taps angry retorts.
The feathers spit, portraying annoyance,
While I listen to the gurgle of an idle engine.
Smoke columns foreshadow red traffic signals,
Emulating from stationary cars; exhausted,
Excreting pungent mist.
A siren cry, a petulant bike, pedestrians scream on by.
The world is against me, I'm buried alive
In a tin coffin, the glass teasing the outside.
I watch the sun dance across the horizon,
Throw back my head in dismay.
Measuring my progress in miniscule microns
Leads my brain cells to begin a decay.

Late Again

"It will be here soon don't worry, don't look so dismayed,
If you're late to work you will still get paid!"

Yet still there's no sign, no tell-tale sound,
The train is late again and rain floods the ground.

Winter is great, so dark and so bleak,
Sat freezing in coats while our emotions peak.

"Where is it??" We ask, teeth gritted and tense.
"I really need know, I can't take this suspense!"

And then the announcement no-one wanted to hear,
The train has been replaced by a bus, for the 5th time this year.

How To Choose Your Tea

Yorkshire or Tetley's or those damned PG Tips,
How do you choose what should pass through your lips?

Some like it bitter or with a slight reddish hue,
While those who like sugar may think you don't have a clue.

Do you stir in the milk or leave it to brew?
Could consider the options 'til your face turns blue!

To me it is easy, how else could it be?
There's but one solution, drink coffee!

The Snowstorm

A furious blizzard or a sprinkling of powder,
One flake on the ground and we couldn't be prouder.
It's funny to think what other countries get,
When all the snow here is pathetic and wet.

It falls for ten minutes and then washes away,
Yet cars still tail back on every motorway.
"Take caution!" we cry, "Do not leave your home!"
We all suffer the same melodrama syndrome.

And then it is gone just as quick as it came,
And weather forecasters bear the brunt of the blame.
Three inches they said, all we have is mush,
We've barely even blinked before it's miserable slush.

Adulthood

A porcelain graveyard, overgrown with weed,
A crystal mirror maze, telling of our greed.

Stainless steel sculpture, balanced and left
To stand there eternal, to wait with bated breath

For a saviour of sorts, a culinary Messiah,
Someone to rekindle a once roaring fire.

Yet I sit and write metaphor instead of getting the job done,
Trying desperately to write pun after pun

While I listen tediously to the sound of a kettle brewing.
I really should man up and accept it. The dishes need doing.

The Commute

Red glare seems to stream right into my face,
Yellow blinking looks nothing but haze.
Tail lights. All I see are tail lights.
I've been driving so long that day turned to night.

A crack in your bumper is a welcome distraction,
Boredom set in a long time ago.
A rare anomaly diverting my mind,
Keeping it vibrant and letting thoughts flow.

It's tiresome you see living life on the road,
As I continue to travel back to my abode.
A soundtrack plays constant, my speakers blare out.
Sometimes I sing and sometimes I just shout.

Now the traffic flows but I know it won't last,
Call me a cynic but I know from the past,
It's a matter of time before things get misled,
Oh, what's that I see! A sign, "Road Closed Ahead"

Caught In A Pickle

I cannot imagine worse,
Than eating my lunch and to find such a curse,

Laying there loathed between slices of cheese,
Staring me right in the face and I freeze!

"What a pickle!" you might say, "What a turn of events!"
To find a whole pickle on this sandwich I've spent,

My own hard-earned cash just to feel discontent,
That green little pickle with its vinegary scent.

Call it pickle a gherkin or the devil's own snack,
I'm taking its presence as a personal attack.

Why would I want this it just tastes so drab?
Can't take one more bite, it's making me gag!

Mutual Friend

When we first spoke, you were but a ghost,
A phantom of sorts commenting on the same post,

A mutual love of the same things arose,
As we began to bond through digital prose.

When we next spoke, you were closer to me,
Not quite in presence but in heart and esprit.

It seemed we were friends and strongly connecting,
Our views and opinions strongly intersecting.

And then when we spoke, it was with great ease,
Like bread spread with butter and pods full of peas.

We're there for each other, whether near or far,
Proof friendship can form anywhere, no matter how bizarre.

A Chimp With A Paddle

A chimp with a paddle firing plastic balls at me,
A chimp with a paddle, serving with glee.

His monkeyish laugh ringing loud in the air,
Standing up hair as he returns the ball with flair.

But then comes disaster as he misses his mark,
Losing his focus as the ball takes an arc,

Straight into the netting and down goes his bat,
A chimp with a paddle, "I quit!" He spat.

The Boot On The Wire

Like a hypnotic pendulum you swing as if weightless;
Trapped for eternity on your wiry perch,
An insulated prison, which your lace intertwines.
You're nothing if not hopeless, an inanimate lost cause,
Eroded by the elements, your colour faded long ago.

While a small bird pecks at your tongue you sit there idle,
Allowing it to tear at the worn leathery skin.
You're beaten and battered, falling apart,
Your soles bear no soul and nobody cares.
You're tossed from a street that has forgotten you're there.

The Splinter

A malicious stake wedged into my finger,
A nightmare in the flesh, buried in skin.
While I try to ignore it, still the pain lingers,
Wincing and moaning, I won't let it win.

The angered red surface on my left hand,
Plays host to the splinter picked up from a tree.
The tweezers won't grab it as I carefully planned,
I struggle and grab but still it won't flee!

Watery eyes and ear-splitting scream,
It begins to anger me and fresh tears pour.
This is like something straight from a bad dream,
I've never known something so awfully sore!

Acknowledgments

I would like to thank the following people for helping this dream to come true. Without them this book would never been a possibility:
To Katie, the love of my life, I thank you for your continued support and inspirational manner, for allowing me the time to write and coping with my insecure, testing self; to my incredible mother and sister, who have guided me through the darkest times in my life; to Nicole, the reason I started this venture in the first place; to Brad, an unorthodox pillar of support found in the strangest of places; Sam, for weighing in honest and invaluable help; I also couldn't forget the unbelievably talented Rishikant Patra for his incredible visuals – I could not have dreamed for better cover artwork; to Ellis, for your toddling influential mayhem.
I give thanks to every poet, companion and friend who has offered support, comfort and advice along this journey; finally, I thank the world for reminding me love and passion exist as well as tolerating my poetic ramblings.